Draw

Dogs

JEREMY MORGAN

Series editors: David and Brenda Herbert

A & C Black • London

First published 1981
New style of paperback binding 1996
by A&C Black (Publishers)
37 Soho Square
London W1D 3QZ

Reprinted 2001

ISBN 0-7136-6238-7

Printed in Hong Kong by Wing King Tong

Cover photograph by Zul Mukhida

Contents

Making a start

Learning to draw is largely a matter of practice and observation—so draw as much and as often as you can, and use your eyes all the time. Watch your dog as it sleeps, eats, stretches, runs around, until you become really familiar with its shape and movements.

Carry a sketchbook with you whenever possible, and don't be shy of using it in public, either for quick notes to be used later or for a finished drawing. The less you think about how you are drawing and the more you think about what you are drawing, the better your drawing will be.

The best equipment will not itself make you a better artist—a masterpiece can be drawn with a stump of pencil on a scrap of paper. But good equipment is encouraging and pleasant to use, so buy the best you can afford and don't be afraid to use it freely.

Experiment with the biggest piece of paper and the boldest, softest piece of chalk or crayon you can find, filling the paper with lines to get a feeling of freedom. Even if you think you have a gift for tiny delicate line drawings with a fine pen or pencil, this is worth trying. It will act as a 'loosening up' exercise. The results may surprise you.

Be self-critical. If a drawing looks wrong, scrap it and start again. Remember that it may take three or four attempts before a drawing looks correct; but keep working at it, because each time you draw you are learning more about your subject. Try to avoid using your eraser too often, and when a line or shape looks right don't overwork it, or your drawing may lose its freshness and liveliness.

What to draw with

SOFT CHISEL PENCIL

4B PENCIL

B

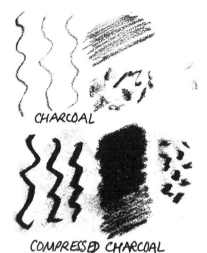

CHARCOAL

COMPRESSED CHARCOAL

PEN & INK

Pencils are graded according to hardness, from 6H (the hardest) through 5H, 4H, 3H, 2H to H; then HB; then B, through 1B, 2B, 3B, 4B, 5B to 6B (the softest). For most purposes, a soft pencil (HB or softer) is best. If you keep it sharp, it will draw as fine a line as a hard pencil but with less pressure, which makes it easier to control. You can soften a line by smudging it with your finger or an eraser, but if you do this too much the drawing will look woolly. A fine range of graphite drawing pencils is Royal Sovereign.

Charcoal is available in three main forms. Royal Sovereign make a charcoal pencil range which is quite dense but dry and produces a dark line or tone. Willow charcoal is the most widely used; it comes in various thicknesses and is very soft and easily smudged and good for large, bold sketches. Compressed charcoal is very dense and the blackest of the three. Charcoal drawings should be sprayed with fixative to prevent smudging.

Wax crayons are hard, greasy and dense, and difficult to erase.

Oil pastels are soft, greasy crayons, available in a wide range of colours.

Chinagraph is a soft, greasy pencil which allows a reasonably fine, dark line or can be used for areas of tone; also available in a variety of colours.

Conté crayons, wood-cased or in solid sticks, are available in various degrees of hardness, and in three colours—black, red and white. They are good for fine line or tonal drawings.

Pastels are soft, dry sticks in a wide range of colours which blend and smudge easily. They are good for quick drawings or large areas of tone. Pastels drawings should be fixed.

Pens vary as much as pencils or crayons.

Mapping pens are only suitable for delicate detail and minute cross-hatching.

Special artists' pens, such as Gillott 303 and Gillott 404, allow you a more varied line, according to the angle at which you

FINE FIBRE PEN

BROAD
FIBRE PEN

hold them and the pressure you use. The Gillot 659 is a very popular crowquill pen.

Reed, bamboo and quill pens are good for bold lines and you can make the nib end narrower or wider with the help of a sharp knife or razor blade. This kind of pen has to be dipped frequently into the ink.

Fountain pens are convenient and portable, but the fixed nib restricts the quality of line.

Special fountain pens, such as Rapidograph and Rotring, control the flow of ink by means of a needle valve in a fine tube (the nib). Nibs are available in several grades of fineness and are interchangeable. (The line they produce is of even thickness, but on coarse paper you can draw an interesting broken line similar to that of a crayon. These pens have to be held at a right-angle to the paper, which is a disadvantage.)

Inks also vary. Waterproof Indian ink quickly clogs the pen. Pelikan Fount India, which is nearly as black, flows more smoothly and does not leave a varnishy deposit on the pen. Ordinary fountain-pen or writing inks (black, blue, green or brown) are less opaque and can give a drawing more variety of tone. You can mix water with any ink in order to make it thinner. But if you are using Indian ink, add distilled or rain water, because ordinary water will cause it to curdle.

Ball point pens are very useful for sketching and quick drawings, but they do not produce a variable line.

Fibre pens are slightly more fluid, but again it is difficult to vary the line.

Brushes can produce a wide variety of marks. Sable or Japanese brushes are the best for drawing because they are very soft and versatile. You can lay a tonal wash of diluted ink over pencil, ink or crayon drawings.

Mixed methods are often pleasing. Try making drawings with pen and pencil, pen and wash or Conté and wash. And try drawing with a pen on wet paper.

What to draw on

Try as many different surfaces as possible.

Ordinary, inexpensive paper is often as good as anything else: for example, brown and buff wrapping paper (Kraft paper) and lining for wallpaper have surfaces which are particularly suitable for charcoal and soft crayons. Some writing and duplicating papers are best for pen drawings. But there are many papers and brands made specially for the artist.

Bristol board is a smooth, hard white board designed for fine pen work.

Ledger Bond paper (cartridge in the UK), the most usual drawing paper, is available in a variety of surfaces—smooth, 'not surface' (semi-rough), rough.

Watercolour papers also come in various grades of smoothness. They are thick, high-quality papers, expensive but pleasant to use.

Ingres paper is mainly for pastel drawings. It has a soft, furry surface and is made in many light colours—grey, pink, blue, buff, etc.

Sketchbooks made up from nearly all these papers, are available. Choose one with thin, smooth paper to begin with. Thin paper means more pages, and a smooth surface is best to record detail.

Lay-out pads make useful sketchbooks. Although their covers are not stiff, you can easily insert a stiff piece of card to act as firm backing to your drawing. The paper is semi-transparent, but this can be useful—almost as tracing paper—if you want to make a new, improved version of your last drawing.

Perspective

You can be an artist without knowing anything about perspective. But most beginners want to know something about it in order to make their drawings appear three-dimensional, so here is a short guide.

The further away an object or part of an object is, the smaller it seems.

All parallel horizontal lines at right-angles to your line of vision remain parallel.

All horizontal lines that are in fact parallel but go away from you will appear to converge at eye-level at the same vanishing point on the horizon. Lines that are above your eye-level will seem to run downwards towards the vanishing point; lines that are below your eye-level will run upwards. You can check the angles of these lines against a pencil held horizontally at eye-level.

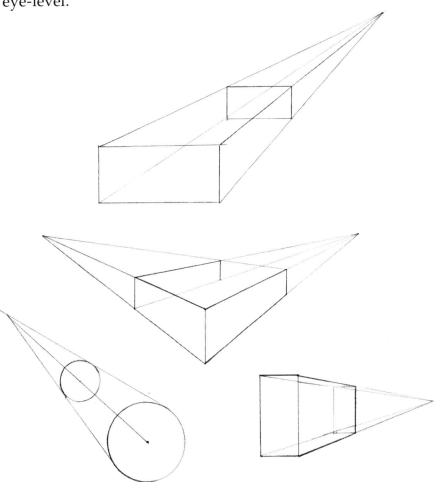

If you look at a dog from different angles, you will notice that its shape seems to change, depending on your viewpoint and the dog's position. The part of the animal closest to you will appear bigger in relation to the part farthest away. Its actual shape will be distorted, or foreshortened.

It is important to draw the shape as it appears from your viewpoint rather than as you know it actually is. You can check the apparent size or depth of any part of your subject by holding a pencil at eye-level and marking the proportion on it with your thumb. Then compare this measurement with that of other parts or areas.

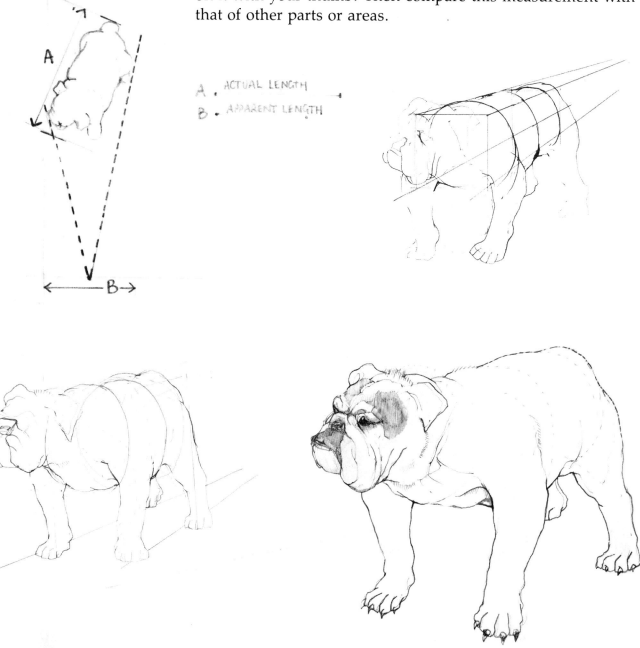

A . ACTUAL LENGTH
B . APPARENT LENGTH

In these drawings, notice that the apparent length from nose to tail is much shorter in relation to the whole animal than it would be if you looked at the dog from the side, when you would see its actual length. Compare the distance between the front legs with that from the shoulder to the rump—from this viewpoint they are roughly the same, although you know that in fact the former is much shorter.

Keep checking the relative proportions and angles of the different parts of your subject in this way, as you draw; compare overall height with overall width, width of head with distance from nose to ear, length and angle of leg against those of the body. You will then get the foreshortening right in your drawing, and the perspective will look right too.

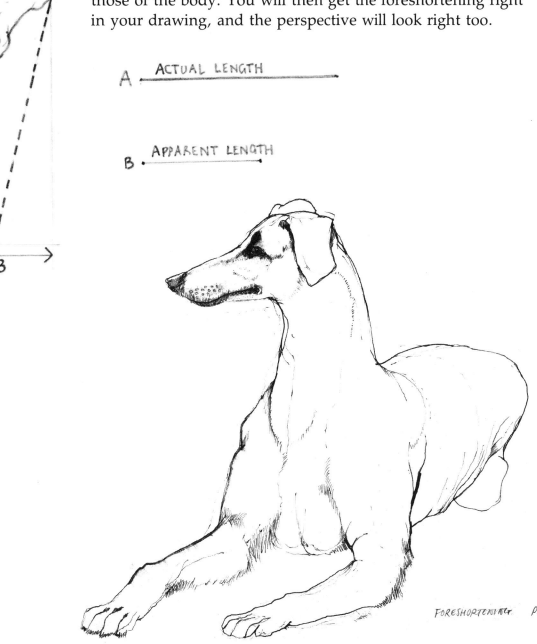

A ___ACTUAL LENGTH___

B ___APPARENT LENGTH___

FORESHORTENING p

Composition

It is important to consider how you want to compose your drawing, that is, how you will place it on your paper. The character of your drawing will be affected by its scale and composition.

Remember, as you look at your subject, that your range of vision is very large in relation to the size of your paper.

A simple aid to composition can be made from a sheet of stiff card, small enough to hold easily in one hand. Cut out a rectangle in the same proportion as your sheet of paper, and look at your subject through this 'frame'. By moving it around you can then decide how much of your subject and the surroundings you want to include and how you will position the drawing on the paper.

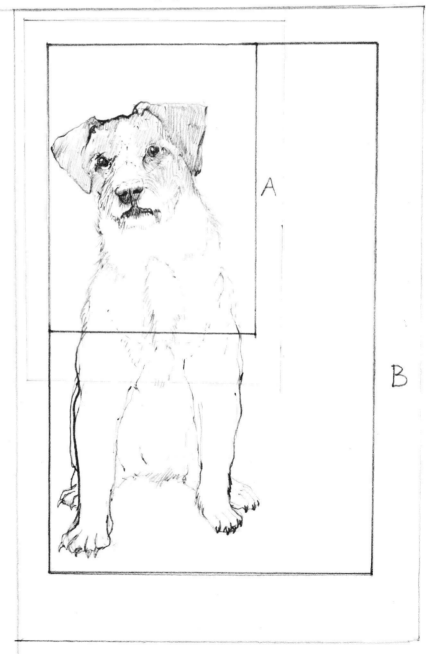

Drawing from a photograph

Drawing from a good-quality photograph can help you to understand the general shapes and proportions.

Make a tracing of your photograph and draw over it a grid of regularly spaced lines. Then draw another grid on your sheet of paper, enlarged or reduced to the same scale. You can now transfer the outline shapes from the tracing to the paper, using the grid as a guide.

It is important to remember that although the photographic image is flat, you should try to make your drawing appear three-dimensional. Notice how the light falls on the various features and use this to indicate volume and shape.

Remember, too, that this method is only to help you start drawing if you do not have a live subject. Try to draw from life whenever you can. Constant observation and practice will help you to learn about your subject and improve your ability.

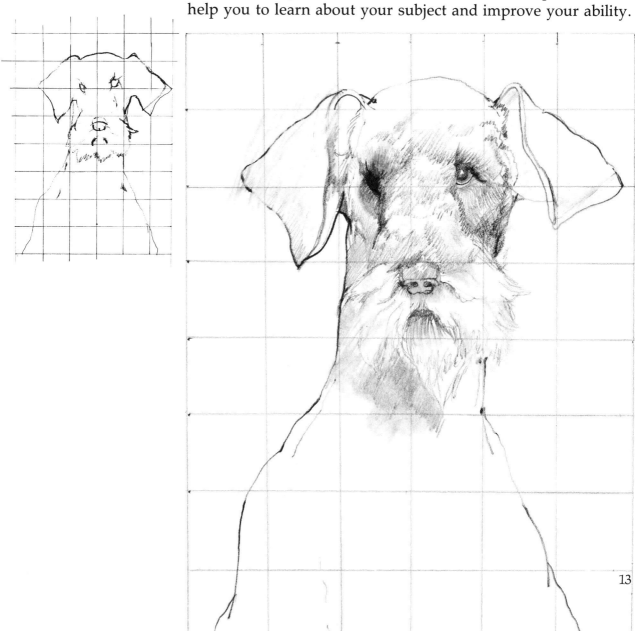

13

Anatomy

A basic knowledge of the dog's anatomy will help you to understand the exterior shape. For instance, the joint half way up the back leg is really the heel, and the joint above it corresponds to the human knee. Notice the relative positions of the other joints, the shape of the rib-cage and the angle of the shoulder-blade.

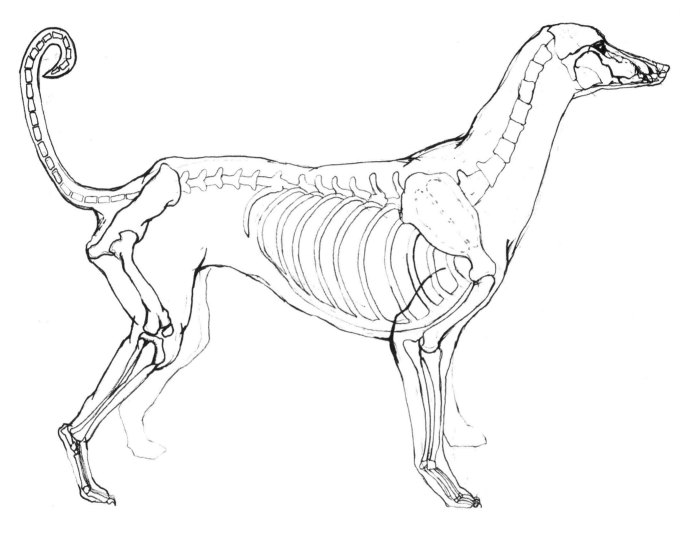

In the second drawing opposite, notice how the muscles are folded round the skeleton. Watch a smooth-haired dog in action to see how its joints and muscles move.

By studying the animal's structure in this way you will be able to make your drawing more accurate and therefore more realistic.

Basic shapes

Look at the overall shape of your subject and the character it conveys. Watch how the muscles tense up when a dog is alert or in movement, and how the shape alters completely when a dog sits down.

When drawing a dog, notice that it is made up of different parts held together by joints and muscles covered by skin and hair. Try to see the shapes created by these bones and muscles.

Remember that all the parts of the body are three-dimensional, and try to suggest this in your drawing. It may help to draw in the contour lines in order to illustrate the volume of the different parts. You can either erase them as you complete the drawing or work over them when you add tone.

Heads

Dogs' heads vary widely in shape, but there are two basic types: the short, snub-nosed head and the longer, narrower head.

When you begin to draw, look for the basic shapes. Look at your subject from different viewpoints and angles to help you understand the shapes you are going to draw.

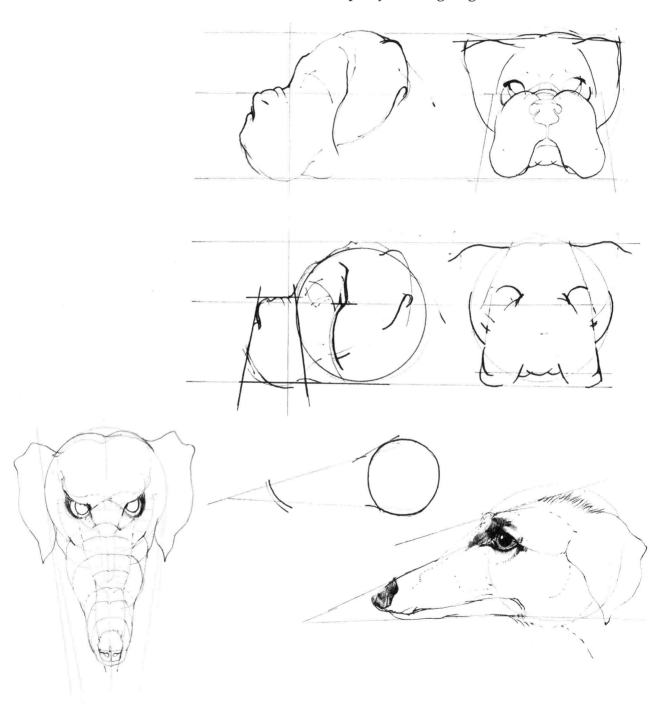

Noses

Notice how the nostrils are folded, how the flesh hangs over the edge at each side. The shape of the nose varies with different breeds.

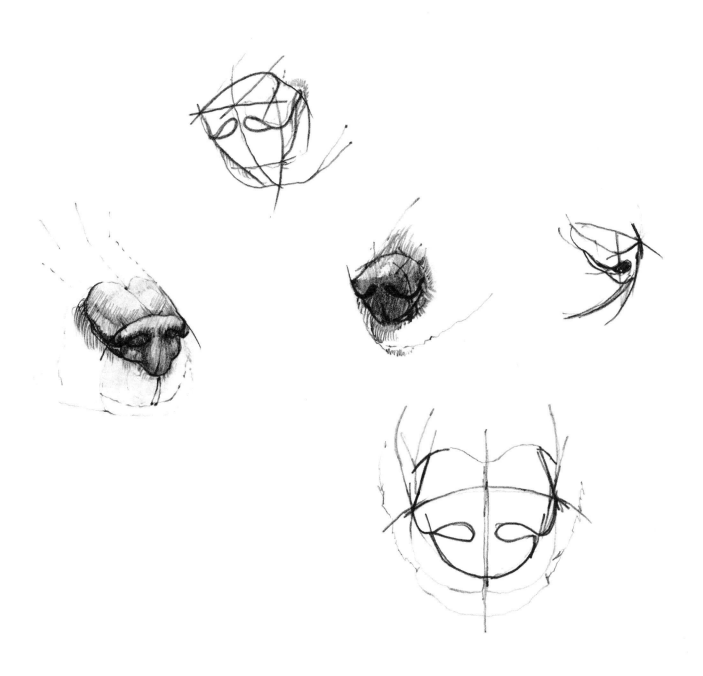

Ears

The shape and proportion of the ears give a dog character and individuality. They may be small and erect, long and floppy, rough or smooth. Notice their structure and how they grow out of the head. Their position also conveys mood and expression.

Eyes

The eyes are the most expressive feature, so spend some time studying them and drawing them.

Remember that the eye is a sphere, of which only a small part is exposed. It is mobile and very fragile and is protected by a part of the skull above it and the muscles around it.

Pay careful attention to the folds of skin which also have a protective function and which affect the shape of the eye. Look for the position of the highlight on the eyeball.

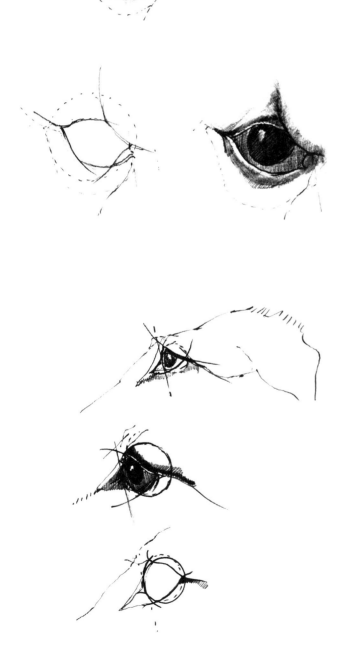

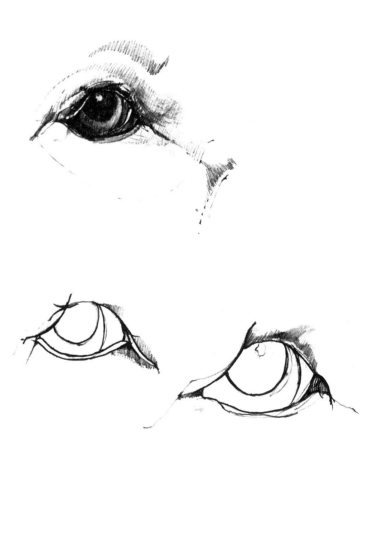

Legs and feet

The legs are also an important part of the character of your subject.

Remember that the legs and feet support all the weight of a standing dog; look carefully at the angles, and observe how the paws spread out as the animal stands firmly on the ground. Compare the characteristically loose and folded skin of a puppy's legs with that an adult dog.

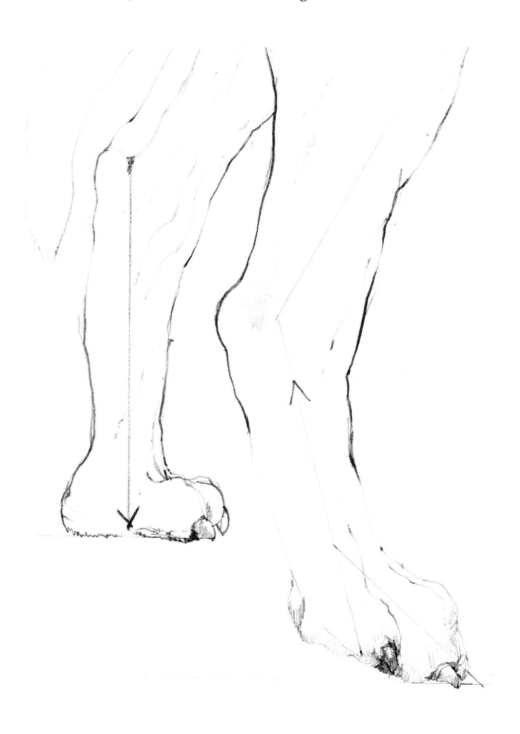

Step by step: the head

The basic shape of this long-nosed mongrel is a cone with a half-sphere (the main skull cavity) at its base. The surface of the cone is broken up into different facets or planes (for example, A, B and C on my drawing).

Begin by lightly drawing the basic shapes. Notice how they change if the head moves to one side or the other. Then study specific areas—around the eyes, the top of the skull, the nose. Look for the different planes and the points where the surface changes direction. Keep moving across the drawing, from one part to another, so that you begin to understand the structure.

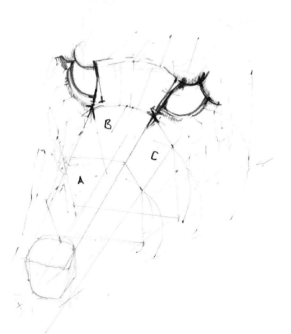

Next begin to work on specific areas in more detail—the shape of the eyes, nose and ears.

Finally, to give your drawing a feeling of solidity, put in the tonal quality—the areas of light and shade across the surface and around the forms, and the way in which the hair lies.

You can follow this same sequence with any shape of head.

Step by step: the whole dog

Observe carefully the posture and the relative proportions of head, body and legs.

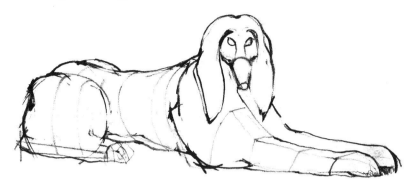

Think about what aspect you want to project. As you draw, look continuously at your subject and notice the particular shapes and characteristics.

Begin by drawing very freely the overall shape. Look for curves, horizontal and vertical lines. Notice how one part flows into another, and the rhythm of the lines.

Then look more carefully at how the individual parts relate: notice how and where the legs emerge from the trunk, how the rib cage hangs, the line of the neck, and how the muscles affect the outline. Try to draw exactly what you see—don't invent lines that you think should be there.

All these observations will help you to understand the underlying structure and make your drawing look three-dimensional. When the basic shapes are right you can add tone and detail.

Proportion

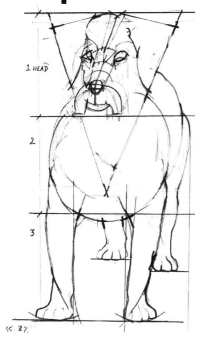

To draw well, you must be constantly aware of the relative proportions of your subject.

One way to check proportion is to use the head as a unit of measurement. Hold your pencil verticallly at arm's length, with the top of the pencil in line with the top of the dog's head, then place your thumb on the pencil in line with the chin. Keeping your thumb in position, work out how many times this head measurement fits into the overall height. This animal's head is one-third of the total height.

Remember, though, that the relative size of the head will differ with the breed of dog and the position in which you draw it.

By holding your pencil vertically, at right angles to the ground, you can also check the angles of the body and legs. This will help to give your drawing accuracy and character.

Action

Your interest may wane if you draw dogs only in standing or sitting positions. Try sketching your dog as it eats, stretches or scratches. Then take your sketchbook into the park or garden and watch your dog running around and meeting other dogs.

Don't attempt clean, finished drawings to start with. Draw freely in soft pencil, charcoal or ink. If you don't succeed at first, start again, and keep on trying.

Look at the basic lines of the neck, shoulder and spine, and notice how they alter as the dog moves. Draw in these lines to record what you have observed.

Remember that the legs of a standing or moving animal bear its weight, and that the distribution of weight alters as it moves. Observe the shift of body weight and how the animal maintains its balance. Notice how it carries its tail.

Continual watching and drawing will increase your understanding and help you to record more accurately what you see.

Materials and techniques

As you draw, you will become aware of the variety of shape, size, colouring and texture in different types of dog. You may find that the materials you use for drawing one dog will be less suitable for drawing another.

Experiment with different media to find new ways of achieving various effects in your drawing. This will make your work more interesting.

Be careful, though, not to become too interested in technique alone. It can be used as an aid to help you achieve the result you want, but remember that observation is the surest way to improve your drawing skill.

Try to use whatever media you choose in as many ways as possible; for example, a pencil that draws a sharp line can also be held at an angle and used for shading.

Experiment on a sheet of paper to discover the variety of marks you can make with one drawing tool. This will be useful when you want to combine different media in one drawing. For example, a pencil used for shading may not produce a dark enough tone for certain features such as the eyes, so try using Conté or chinagraph to give the depth of tone you want.

Discover different ways of conveying the texture of different types of hair—a sharp pencil, or pen and ink, for short wiry hair, charcoal for long, soft hair, etc.

The following pages show examples of the use of different media.

These two heads were drawn with a fine pen and black ink, using a 2B pencil for shading.

Quick sketches made
with a fine felt-tip pen.

To draw the texture of long hair you can use charcoal and an eraser. Draw lines to show how the hair lies over the body, then gently rub with the edge of the eraser to get tonal and textural effects.

This bulldog was drawn with wax crayon and pencil.

A thick felt marker can be
used for quick, bold
drawing but is not good
for detail.

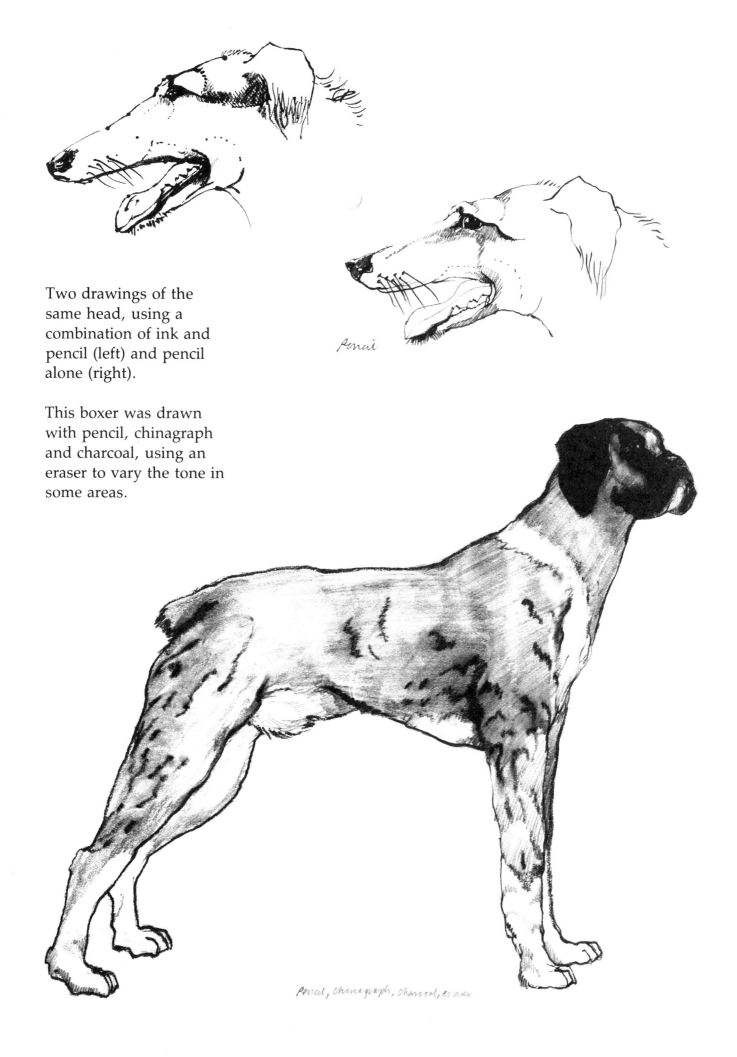

Two drawings of the same head, using a combination of ink and pencil (left) and pencil alone (right).

This boxer was drawn with pencil, chinagraph and charcoal, using an eraser to vary the tone in some areas.

Pencil

Pencil, chinagraph, charcoal, eraser

You can draw on
coloured paper, using
black and white pastels,
and the paper will
provide a third tone.

If you draw with ink on wet paper, the lines will blur to give a soft, furry effect. Additional sharp lines can be added when the paper is dry.

A combination of pen
and ink, pencil and wash
is a good way to convey
the effect of colour
variation in your subject.

This drawing and the one
opposite were done with
a soft wax pencil, with
the addition of a 4B
pencil for shading.

This terrier was drawn with a 4B pencil. Remember to sharpen your pencil frequently to keep the lines crisp and give your drawing sensitivity.

Here I have used 2B and
4B pencils, with charcoal
pencil for the darkest
areas.

A pencil drawing rubbed
with a French stick.